31.00

PROFESSIONAL ESPORTS LEAGUES

ESPORTS LIVE

JOSH GREGORY

CHERRY LAKE PRESS

Published in the United States of America by Cherry Lake Publishing Group
Ann Arbor, Michigan
www.cherrylakepublishing.com

Reading Adviser: Marla Conn, MS, Ed., Literacy specialist, Read-Ability, Inc.
Photo Credits: © Athitat Shinagowin/Shutterstock.com, cover, 1; © ESL [Bart Oerbekke], 5, 10; © ESL [Stephania Lieske], 6; © ESL [Helena Kristiansson], 8, 13, 14, 17, 20, 25, 26; © ESL [Adela Sznajder], 9, 21; © Barone Firenze/Shutterstock.com, 18; © Lauren Elisabeth/Shutterstock.com, 19; © Roman Kosolapov/Shutterstock.com, 22; © ESL [Stephanie Lindgren], 28

Cherry Lake Press is an imprint of Cherry Lake Publishing Group.

Library of Congress Cataloging-in-Publication Data

Names: Gregory, Josh, author.
Title: Professional esports leagues / by Josh Gregory.
Description: Ann Arbor, Michigan : Cherry Lake Publishing, 2021. | Series: Esports live | Includes index. | Audience: Grades 4-6
Identifiers: LCCN 2020002826 (print) | LCCN 2020002827 (ebook) | ISBN 9781534168855 (hardcover) | ISBN 9781534170537 (paperback) | ISBN 9781534172371 (pdf) | ISBN 9781534174214 (ebook)
Subjects: LCSH: Electronic games—Juvenile literature. | Professional sports—Juvenile literature.
Classification: LCC GV1469.15 .G745 2020 (print) | LCC GV1469.15 (ebook) | DDC 794.806—dc23
LC record available at https://lccn.loc.gov/2020002826
LC ebook record available at https://lccn.loc.gov/2020002827

Cherry Lake Publishing Group would like to acknowledge the work of the Partnership for 21st Century Learning, a Network of Battelle for Kids. Please visit http://www.battelleforkids.org/networks/p21 for more information.

Printed in the United States of America
Corporate Graphics

ABOUT THE AUTHOR

Josh Gregory is the author of more than 150 books for kids. He has written about everything from animals to technology to history. A graduate of the University of Missouri–Columbia, he currently lives in Chicago, Illinois.

TABLE OF CONTENTS

CHAPTER 1

Getting Organized

If you like to play or watch video games, you're probably already familiar with the world of **esports**. Some of the best video game players face off in thrilling, head-to-head competitions. Winners can walk away with fame, fans, and a whole lot of money. Matches are often dramatic, exciting events where huge crowds of fans pack arenas to cheer on their favorite players. Meanwhile, millions more enjoy the action from home by watching on their favorite streaming services. It's a lot of fun to follow along and keep up with the latest developments.

Not all esports organizations are leagues. Some are simply companies that host various stand-alone tournaments.

    Esports events are different from the online video game matches you might play with friends. They are not casual events where people play for fun. They are carefully planned and organized. Most of the time, players have to prove themselves before they are allowed to participate.

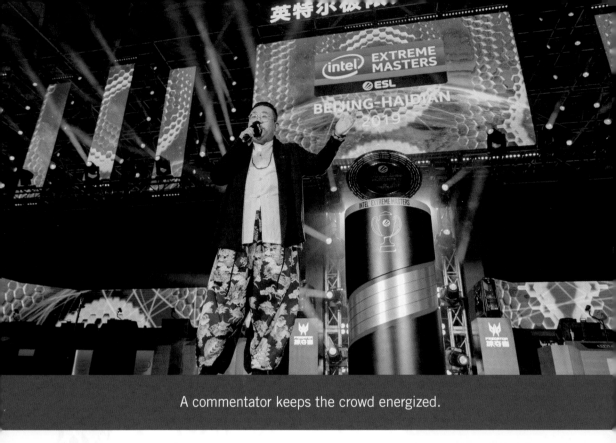

A commentator keeps the crowd energized.

Many professional esports competitions are overseen by organizations called leagues. If you watch traditional sports, you probably have some idea of what a league is. A typical league is an organization that oversees a group of teams or players. The teams or individuals in this group regularly face off against each other in a series of matches called a season. At the end of the season, the players with the best records compete in a final set of playoff matches to determine who will be the champion.

The teams in a league are usually somewhat independent. They are allowed to recruit players and plan strategies as they see fit. But the league sets rules that each team must follow. It also schedules matches and performs the many other jobs needed to hold a pro esports event.

A lot of hard work goes into each and every event. Esports organizations have a lot going on behind the scenes. First, they need to decide when and where the tournament will take place. They need to find a **venue** that is able to host the event. They need to think about the number of seats, the type of equipment needed, and the cost of the venue.

The organizers will also need to hire people to help them run the event. A typical pro esports match has **commentators** to help explain the action to fans and make matches more exciting. Tech people make sure all of the computers and other equipment used in a match stay working correctly. There are often experts on-site to keep an eye out for cheating in matches.

INTEL° EXTREME MASTERS   CH

Fans are excited to see their favorite players and teams.

Once the event itself has been carefully planned, the organizers need to consider how they will **promote** it. They need to find ways to advertise and generate excitement for the event online. They also need to think about how it will be streamed online. They can **broadcast** through Twitch, YouTube, and other services. Or they can make a deal to exclusively stream the event from one place.

Teams play for huge cash prizes and trophies.

The trophy and a team's stats are prominently displayed during a tournament.

Many of an esports organization's responsibilities revolve around money. The organizers need to make sure they have enough money to pay for the expenses of setting up the event. The costs of running a big tournament can add up quickly. Most events promise big cash prizes to the winners. And of course, the organizers' goal is probably to make money from their event.

This means that they need to figure out ways to bring in more cash while keeping costs as low as they can. They set ticket prices for people coming to see the event live. They might also sell merchandise such as T-shirts. A lot of money comes from advertising and **sponsorships**. All kinds of companies pay esports organizers to display logos for their products at events.

If all goes according to plan, the event will proceed smoothly. Everyone will have a good time, and the organizers can get to work planning their next competition.

Something for Everyone

There is no single organization that oversees all of esports. Instead, there are many different leagues, teams, and other groups. Each one has its own way of doing things. The way one tournament is organized might be completely different from another. This can make it tough for new fans to figure out just what is going on in the world of esports. But it also means there is a lot of variety. No matter what you are into, there is probably an esports competition you would like.

CHAPTER 2

Rules and Regulations

Any fair, organized competition needs a strict set of rules for players and teams to follow. Well-designed rules make it harder for any player to gain an unfair advantage over others. They also ensure that matches are fun and exciting for fans to watch.

Most games allow players to adjust various options and settings. For example, a fighting game might allow players to decide whether each round of a match lasts 30 seconds or 60 seconds. In competitive play, it is up to esports organizers to decide which settings are best. Often, many players and organizations will agree that certain rules and settings work best for certain games. They will stay **consistent** across most pro competitions. Other times, there

Pro esports players are monitored very closely during a competition.

might be a lot of debate over what is the most fair and fun way to play a certain game.

Other rules determine how matches are scored and how players progress to more advanced rounds of a tournament. Questions like how many players will be allowed to compete in an event, how they will be selected, and what to do in case of a tie, are also answered. These things all need to be decided ahead of time and clearly communicated to players.

Just like in any other sport, team spirit and sportsmanship
are important in esports.

Some of the strictest rules in any esports competition deal with cheating. Cheating is a big problem in many competitive games. Players sometimes install programs called hacks on their computer. These programs modify a game to give a player advantages over others. For example, they might give players perfect aim or allow them to see through walls. Most esports organizations immediately kick out any players or teams that try to cheat. They might also ban them from participating in future events.

Sometimes, an organization might find that some of its rules aren't working as well as they could. Maybe fans and players have complained about the length of matches in a certain game. Or maybe some players have found a way to make a game unfair, even while following the rules. Esports organizers have to react to these situations and tweak their rules as needed to make sure everything stays fun and fair.

Deciding What to Play

Some esports organizations oversee competition in a number of different games. They don't have to stick to any one title. This means they have to make big decisions about which games will host events. Not every video game is cut out for esports. It needs to be something people will enjoy watching as much as playing. And a pool of skilled players is needed to participate in pro events. Some games go out of style after a while, and new ones are always being created. Organizers have to pay attention to which games are on the rise and which ones aren't drawing quite as many fans anymore.

CHAPTER 3

Leagues, Teams, and Other Organizations

There are many different esports leagues and organizations in business today. Some are small, local operations. Others are massive international companies with fans all over the world.

One of the largest and oldest esports organizations is the Electronic Sports League (ESL). It was formed in Germany in 2000. These days, it is more than just a league. ESL hosts tournaments, championship leagues, and a variety of other competitions all over the world. Its biggest events include the annual Intel Extreme Masters and the ESL One series of tournaments. All kinds of games are played at ESL events, and they change all the time depending on what is popular in the esports community.

The Intel Extreme Masters *Counter-Strike* trophy
is engraved with the names of past winners.

Major League Gaming (MLG) is another big player in the
modern esports scene. Like ESL, it has been around for a while.
MLG was founded in 2002 in New York City. At first, MLG focused
more on console gaming than other esports organizations, which
usually concentrated on PC games. MLG hosted competitions
for shooting games such as the *Halo* and *Call of Duty* series.

Super Smash Bros. is popular because it combines characters from all different worlds and games.

MLG also held pro events for fighting games such as *Tekken* and *Super Smash Bros.* In 2015, the organization was purchased by Activision Blizzard, one of the world's biggest game publishing companies. MLG now focuses entirely on Activision Blizzard games, including *World of Warcraft, StarCraft,* and *Call of Duty.*

Call of Duty was first released in 2003.

Due to global health concerns in early 2020, for the first time ever, the IEM tournament in Katowice, Poland, was closed to the public. The event was still broadcasted live.

Many professional leagues have teams that specialize in certain games.

One organization that does things a little differently is the *Overwatch* League (OWL). OWL was founded in 2017 by Activision Blizzard, and it is run as part of MLG. But unlike most esports competitions, it is set up almost exactly like a traditional sports league. Players compete in just one game: *Overwatch*. Teams are

Team Vitality is a French esports league that started in 2013.
They are one of the leading teams in Europe.

located in different cities around the world. Each has its own home arena, and teams travel to play against each one another. They compete in scheduled matches over the course of a regular season. Then the top teams face off in championship playoff matches.

Esports players benefit in many ways by joining a team. In addition to winning money from competitions, they often earn a regular **salary**. Most teams also have full-time coaches and other employees to assist the players. The biggest esports teams have huge audiences, with millions of fans streaming matches and following them on social media. This means joining a team can lead to an instant fan base.

Signature Sneakers

*In traditional sports, one of the signs that an athlete has hit the big time is when they get a **signature** sneaker. Lately, sneaker companies are starting to collaborate with esports teams. In 2019, Adidas released a new shoe called the AM4 VIT.01. This unique sneaker was a signature design created for Team Vitality. It sold out quickly, so it's probably only a matter of time before other esports teams start getting their own shoe deals.*

CHAPTER 4

The Big Events

The biggest esports competitions are truly massive events. They draw huge crowds of fans. For example, about 174,000 people attended ESL's Intel Extreme Masters World Championship event in 2019. Entire stadiums can sell out in minutes for highly anticipated tournaments. And then there are the millions of people who watch from home on streaming services like Twitch.

One of the most popular yearly events in esports is the International, a *Dota 2* championship held by the game's **developers**, Valve Software. The tournament has been held each year since 2011.

Esports arenas can hold thousands of fans.

There are currently 13 professional esports
organizations in the United States.

Only 18 teams are invited to participate. They are chosen based
on their performance in other *Dota 2* events held earlier in the year.
The International has gotten bigger and bigger every year, and
it is typically broadcast live on national TV.

Similarly popular is the annual *League of Legends* World Championship hosted by Riot Games. Like the International, this competition has been held every year since 2011. Teams come from all over the world, and the event draws a remarkably huge audience. The 2018 tournament broke records when almost 100 million people tuned in to watch on streaming services. Almost as many people tune in to the Super Bowl each year.

For fans of fighting games, the Evolution Championship Series is the most important competition of the year. Known among fans as simply "Evo," it began in 1996 and has been held annually since 2000. Evo is open to anyone who wants to participate. This means that a previously unknown player is able to show up and win the whole thing, even if they have never played in a pro event before. Thousands of fighting game players from all over the world travel to Evo each year to make their mark on the esports community.

Most pro esports players retire in their 20s. Teams are always evolving.

In 2019, Epic Games held the first *Fortnite* World Cup. It immediately became one of the biggest events in esports. Like Evo, it was an open tournament where anyone could participate. The early rounds are held online. The very best players from these weekly competitions are invited to attend the finals: a massive live event held in a stadium. In 2019, more than 40 million people logged on and tried their best to win a spot in the finals.

The future looks bright for esports. More leagues and teams are forming every day. Events are getting bigger and bigger. New fans are joining in the fun all the time. Whatever happens next, it's sure to be amazing.

More and More Money

As the field of esports grows bigger, so do the prizes players can win at major tournaments. In recent years, esports organizations have worked hard to outdo one another with their prize pools. The current record belongs to the International 2019, a Dota 2 tournament. More than $34 million was awarded to the winners. Future events are likely to award players with even higher payouts!

Think About It

Have you ever wanted to play in a video game tournament? Try planning and hosting one yourself. You don't need a stadium full of fans to have a fun competition with friends.

- Figure out ahead of time who is going to compete. Draw a tournament bracket.

- Decide on the rules for your tournament. What game will you play? What settings will you use in the game?

- Make sure everyone plays fair. Most importantly, have a good time!

For More Information

BOOKS

Austic, Greg. *Game Design.* Ann Arbor, MI: Cherry Lake Publishing, 2013.

Reeves, Diane Lindsey. *Find Your Future in Technology.* Ann Arbor, MI: Cherry Lake Publishing, 2016.

Trueit, Trudi Strain. *Video Gaming.* Ann Arbor, MI: Cherry Lake Publishing, 2008.

WEBSITES

Mixer
www.mixer.com
This interactive livestreaming service by Microsoft is home to a few of the biggest names in game streaming.

Twitch
www.twitch.tv
Check out some streams for yourself on the most popular streaming service.

GLOSSARY

broadcast (BRAWD-kast) to transmit video or audio to an audience via radio, TV, or the internet

commentators (KAH-muhn-tay-turz) people who talk about a live sporting event as it happens, to make the event more interesting and exciting for viewers

consistent (kuhn-SIS-tuhnt) always the same

developers (dih-VEL-uh-purz) people who make video games or other computer programs

esports (EE-sports) the sport of professional video game competitions

promote (pruh-MOHT) to spread the word about something

salary (SAL-uh-ree) regular payments made to employees by a company

signature (SIG-nuh-chur) something, like a style or logo, that serves to identify or set apart

sponsorships (SPAHN-sur-ships) arrangements where companies pay to support an event or team, usually in exchange for advertising opportunities

venue (VEN-yoo) a place where events are held

INDEX